Reflections

Sept. 4, 1991

Dear "Sis" —

As I am getting ready for our trip to the Orient, I reflect back on so many things. How I treasure our 62 years friendship and all you mean to me. I want to send you this book and know you will like the verses. It is from a different set than others I sent you.

I love you very much, my "Heart" Sister — could not more if we were really born sisters.

Lib

THE HELEN STEINER RICE FOUNDATION

Whatever the celebration, whatever the day, whatever the event, whatever the occasion, Helen Steiner Rice possessed the ability to express the appropriate feeling for that particular moment in time.

A happening became happier, a sentiment more sentimental, a memory more memorable because of her deep sensitivity to put into understandable language the emotion being experienced. Her positive attitude, her concern for others, and her love of God are identifiable threads woven into her life, her works . . . and even her death.

Prior to her passing, she established the HELEN STEINER RICE FOUNDATION, a nonprofit corporation whose purpose is to award grants to worthy charitable programs that aid the elderly, the needy, and the poor. In her lifetime, these were the individuals about whom Mrs. Rice was greatly concerned.

Royalties from the sale of this book will add to the financial capabilities of the HELEN STEINER RICE FOUNDATION, thus making possible additional grants. Each year this foundation presents grants, ranging from three thousand to fifteen thousand dollars each, to various, qualified, worthwhile, and charitable programs. Because of her foresight, her caring, and her deep convictions, Helen Steiner Rice continues to touch a countless number of lives. Thank you for your assistance in helping to keep Helen's dream alive.

Virginia J. Ruehlmann, Administrator
The Helen Steiner Rice Foundation
Suite 2100, Atrium Two
221 E. Fourth Street
Cincinnati, Ohio 45201

Reflections

Helen Steiner Rice

Prayers by Virginia J. Ruehlmann

CARMEL • NEW YORK 10512

Dedicated to the memory of Helen Steiner Rice.
Her poetic reflections
enrich our lives
and encourage us to appreciate
our many blessings.

Contents

Reflections can take many forms: scenes reproduced in a clear lake, images of one's self in a looking glass, echoes and sounds vibrated from mountaintops, and thoughtful mental analyses. The Bible, God's Word, is a reflection of the truths necessary for successful living.

Helen Steiner Rice's goal was "to never consciously hurt anyone; to do as much good as possible, as often as possible, and in as many places as possible." That goal was a reflection of biblical teaching.

Daily Reflections, the final book in the *Daily* series, completes the seasonal cycle. One's journey of faith does not end, however. It continues, reflecting with each passing year the ongoing process of spiritual growth and the search for inner peace.

Virginia J. Ruehlmann

Reflections of a Thankful Heart

Take nothing for granted
For whenever you do
The joy of enjoying
Is lessened for you.
For we rob our own lives
Much more than you know
When we fail to reflect
Or in anyway show
Our thanks for the blessings
That daily are ours . . .
The warmth of the sun,
The fragrance of flowers,
The kind, little deeds
So thoughtfully done,
The favors of friends
And the love that someone
Unselfishly gives us
In a myriad of ways,
Expecting no payment
And no words of praise—
Oh, great is our loss
When we no longer find
A thankful response
To things of this kind.
For the joy of enjoying
And the fullness of living
Are reflections of the heart
That is filled with thanksgiving.

Prayer

When you pray, go into your room and shut the door
and pray to your Father who is in secret; and your
Father who sees in secret will reward you.

Matthew 6:6

I remember so well this prayer I said
Each night as my mother tucked me in bed,
And today this same prayer is still the best way
To sign off with God at the end of the day
And to ask Him your soul to safely keep
As you wearily close tired eyes in sleep
Feeling content that the Father above
Will hold you secure in His great arms of love . . .
And having His promise that if ere you wake
His angels will reach down your sweet soul to take
Is perfect assurance that awake or asleep
God is always right there to tenderly keep
All of His children ever safe in His care
For God's here and He's there and He's everywhere
So into His hands each night as I sleep
I commit my soul for the dear Lord to keep.

*Do You ever sleep, God? No matter what hour it is when I
awaken or go to sleep, You are with me.*

11

Then you shall call, and the Lord will answer; you
shall cry, and he will say, "Here I am."

Isaiah 58:9

Do you want what you want when you want it?
Do you pray and expect a reply?
And when it's not instantly answered
Do you feel that God passed you by?
Well, prayers that are prayed in this manner
Are really not prayers at all
For you can't go to God in a hurry
And expect Him to answer your call.
For prayers are not meant for obtaining
What we selfishly wish to acquire,
For God in His wisdom refuses
The things that we wrongly desire. . . .
Wake up! You are missing completely
The reason and purpose of prayer,
Which is really to keep us contented
That God holds us safe in His care.
And God only answers our pleadings
When He knows that our wants fill a need
And whenever our will becomes His will
There is no prayer that God does not heed!

*Loving Father, You give so much, and yet I ask for even
more. Instill within me satisfaction for what I do have and
not a longing for what I don't have.*

God, Grant Us Wisdom

And he came to the disciples and found them sleeping; and he said to Peter, "So, could you not watch with me one hour? Watch and pray that you may not enter into temptation; the spirit indeed is willing, but the flesh is weak."

Matthew 26:40, 41

God, grant us the grace to use
all the hours of our days,
Not for our own selfish interests
and our own willful ways,
But teach us to take time for praying
and for listening to You,
So each day is spent wisely,
doing what You want us to do.

Dear God, guide me so that I can evaluate right and wrong. Enable me to put aside selfish wants and desires.

. . . "You shall love your neighbor as yourself." Love does no wrong to a neighbor; therefore love is the fulfilling of the law.

Romans 13:9, 10

Dear God, much too often
　　we seek You in prayer
Because we are wallowing
　　in our own self-despair.
We make every word
　　we lamentingly speak
An imperative plea
　　for whatever we seek.
We pray for ourselves
　　and so seldom for others,
We're concerned with our problems
　　and not with our brothers'.

We seem to forget, Lord,
  that the sweet hour of prayer
Is not for self-seeking
  but to place in Your care
All the lost souls
  unloved and unknown
And to keep praying for them
  until they're Your own.
For it's never enough
  to seek God in prayer
With no thought of others
  who are lost in despair.
So teach us, dear God,
  that the power of prayer
Is made stronger by placing
  the world in Your care!

Gentle Jesus, soften my words. Speak them for me. Father, if I become discontented with others, it can only mean one thing: I am obviously discontented with myself. Help me to discover the reason. Let me deal as gently with the faults of others as I deal with my own. Increase my compassion.

A Prayer for Those We Love

Then they cried to the Lord in their trouble, and he delivered them from their distress; he made the storm be still, and the waves of the sea were hushed. Then they were glad because they had quiet, and he brought them to their desired haven. Let them thank the Lord for his steadfast love, for his wonderful works to the sons of men!

Psalm 107:28–31

"Our Father who art in heaven,"
Hear this little prayer
And reach across the miles today
That stretch from here to there,
So I may feel much closer
To those I'm fondest of
And they may know I think of them
With thankfulness and love,
And help all people everywhere
Who must often dwell apart
To know that they're together
In the haven of the heart!

Our Father, bless and keep my loved ones here, there, and everywhere.

A Little Prayer for You

And whatever you ask in prayer, you will receive, if you have faith.

Matthew 21:22

I said a little prayer for you
        and I asked the Lord above
To keep you safely in His care
And enfold you in His love
I did not ask for fortune
        for riches or for fame
I only ask for blessings
        in the Savior's holy name
Blessings to surround you
        in times of trial and stress
And inner joy to fill your heart
        with peace and happiness.

Is there someone for whom I should be praying today, someone who needs You, Jesus?

Let the word of Christ dwell in you richly, teach and admonish one another in all wisdom, and sing psalms and hymns and spiritual songs with thankfulness in your hearts to God. And whatever you do, in word or deed, do everything in the name of the Lord Jesus, giving thanks to God the Father through him.

Colossians 3:16, 17

There's no problem too big
and no question too small,
Just ask God in faith
and He'll answer them all.
Not always at once,
so be patient and wait,
For God never comes
too soon or too late.
So trust in His wisdom
and believe in His Word,
For no prayer is unanswered
and no prayer unheard.

Father, be with me as I strive to be truthful, trustworthy, and responsible in all my words and actions in every situation.

Don't worry about anything; instead, pray about everything; tell God your needs and don't forget to thank him for his answers.

Philippians 4:6 TLB

> Let us find comfort
>   and strength for each day
> In knowing that Christ
>   walked this same earthly way.
> So whenever we're troubled
>   and lost in despair
> We have but to seek Him
>   and ask Him in prayer
> To guide and direct us
>   and help us to bear
> Our sickness and sorrow,
>   our worry and care.

I shall rejoice because You, God, are always here and You hear even the smallest and quietest of prayers.

Faith

. . . make every effort to supplement your faith with virtue, and virtue with knowledge, and knowledge with self-control, and self-control with steadfastness, and steadfastness with godliness, and godliness with brotherly affection, and brotherly affection with love.

2 Peter 1:5–7

We look ahead through each changing year
With mixed emotions of
Hope and fear,
Hope for the peace we long have sought,
Fear that our hopes
will come to naught . . .
Unwilling to trust in the Father's will,
We count on our logic and shallow skill
And, in our arrogance and pride,
Man is no longer satisfied
To place his confidence and love
With childlike faith
in God above . . .
But tiny hands and tousled heads
That kneel in prayer by little beds
Are closer to the dear Lord's heart
And of His Kingdom
more a part
Than we who search and never find
The answers to our questioning mind.

God, give me an unfailing confidence in You, a childlike trust in You, and a mature faith in Your teachings.

For you have been called for this purpose, since Christ also suffered for you, leaving you an example for you to follow in His steps.

1 Peter 2:21 NAS

> Somebody loves you more than you know,
> Somebody goes with you wherever you go,
> Somebody really and truly cares
> And lovingly listens to all of your prayers.
> Don't doubt for a minute
>   that this is true,
> For God loves His children
>   and takes care of them, too.
> And all of His treasures
>   are yours to share
> If you love Him completely
>   and show Him you care.
> And if you walk in his footsteps
>   and have the faith to believe,
> There's nothing you ask for
>   that you will not receive!

Dear Comforter of all! How consoling and reassuring to realize that at all times You love me and that You care about me.

Now faith is the assurance of things hoped for, the conviction of things not seen.

Hebrews 11:1 NAS

There are many things in life
That we cannot understand,
But we must trust God's judgment
And be guided by His hand,
And all who have God's blessing
Can rest safely in His care
For He promises safe passage
On the wings of faith and prayer.

Keep me resourceful, Lord. Let me view the troubles ahead of me with the knowledge that if I face those troubles with You at my side, I can find a blessing hidden in each one.

You need to keep on patiently doing God's will if you want him to do for you all that he has promised.

Hebrews 10:36 TLB

> Deal only with the present,
> Never step into tomorrow,
> For God asks us just to trust Him
> And to never borrow sorrow.
> For the future is not ours to know
> And it may never be,
> So let us live and give our best
> And give it lavishly.
> For to meet tomorrow's troubles
> Before they are even ours
> Is to anticipate the Savior
> And to doubt His all-wise powers.
> So let us be content to solve
> Our problems one by one,
> Asking nothing of tomorrow
> Except "Thy will be done."

Dear God, let me patiently persevere doing that which You have planned for me to do, and let me realize that Your timing is perfect.

Let all bitterness and wrath and anger and clamor and slander be put away from you, with all malice, and be kind to one another, tenderhearted, forgiving one another, as God in Christ forgave you.

Ephesians 4:31, 32

From one day to another,
    God will gladly give
To everyone who seeks Him
    and tries each day to live
A little bit more closely
    to God and to each other,
Seeing everyone who passes
    as a neighbor, friend, or brother,
Not only joy and happiness
    but the faith to meet each trial
Not with fear and trepidation
    but with an inner smile.
For we know life's never measured
    by how many years we live
But by the kindly things we do
    and the happiness we give.

Jesus, may I always see a person made in Your image in each individual I meet and may I always treat that person as kindly as I wish to be treated.

. . . I trust in God's unfailing love for ever and ever. I will praise you forever for what you have done; in your name I will hope, for your name is good. I will praise you in the presence of your saints.

Psalm 52:8, 9 NIV

Whatever our problems, troubles, and sorrows,
If we trust in the Lord,
    there'll be brighter tomorrows,
For there's nothing too much
    for the great God to do,
And all that He asks or expects from you
Is faith that's unshaken by tribulations and tears
That keeps growing stronger along with the years,
Content in the knowledge that God knows best
And that trouble and sorrow are only a test.
For without God's testing of our soul
It never would reach its ultimate goal.
So keep on believing, whatever betide you,
Knowing that God will be with you to guide you,
And all that He promised will be yours to receive
If you trust Him completely and always believe.

Today is the beginning of forever. I shall start this day by trusting solely and soully in You, Lord. I shall not question even one happening. I shall accept what comes my way with complete faith in You.

And he said to him, "You shall love the Lord your God with all your heart, and with all your soul, and with all your mind."

Matthew 22:37

God, help me in my feeble way
To somehow do something each day
To show You that I love You best
And that my faith will stand each test
And let me serve You every day
And feel You near me when I pray . . .
Oh, hear my prayer, dear God above,
And make me worthy of Your love!

Dear God, what can I do to translate Your love into action in all that I do today? Let my love echo and re-echo, resounding through the tasks that I undertake.

Cast your burden on the Lord, and he will sustain you; he will never permit the righteous to be moved.

Psalm 55:22

Remember me, God?
I come every day
Just to talk with You, Lord,
And to learn how to pray.
You make me feel welcome,
You reach out Your hand,
I need never explain
For You understand.
I come to You frightened
And burdened with care
So lonely and lost
And so filled with despair,
And suddenly, Lord,
I'm no longer afraid,
My burden is lighter
And the dark shadows fade.
Oh, God, what a comfort
To know that You care
And to know when I seek You
You will always be there!

Whatever happens to me today, let me react in a manner that is pleasing to You, God.

So if we say we are his friends, but go on living in spiritual darkness and sin, we are lying. But if we are living in the light of God's presence, just as Christ does, then we have wonderful fellowship and joy with each other, and the blood of Jesus his Son cleanses us from every sin.

1 John 1:6, 7 TLB

In this sick world of hatred
And violence and sin,
Where men renounce morals
And reject discipline,
We stumble in darkness
Groping vainly for light
To distinguish the difference
Between wrong and right,
But dawn cannot follow
This night of despair
Unless faith lights a candle
In all hearts everywhere.
And warmed by the glow
Our hate melts away
And love lights the path
To a peaceful, new day.

Light of the World, how much wiser and better it is for me to light one small candle than to dread and fear the darkness. Light of the World, let Your light and Your love be in me and with me and shine through me.

Love

As the Father has loved me, so have I loved you; abide in my love. If you keep my commandments, you will abide in my love, just as I have kept my Father's commandments and abide in his love. These things I have spoken to you, that my joy may be in you, and that your joy may be full. This is my commandment, that you love one another as I have loved you.

John 15:9–12

"Love one another as I have loved you"
May seem impossible to do.
But if you will try to trust and believe,
Great are the joys that you will receive.
For love makes us patient, understanding, and kind,
And we judge with our heart and not with our mind.
For as soon as love enters the heart's opened door,
The faults we once saw are not there anymore.
And the things that seemed wrong begin to
     look right
When viewed in the softness of love's gentle light.
For love works in ways that are wondrous
     and strange
And there is nothing in life that love cannot change,
And all that God promised will someday come true
When you love one another the way He loves you.

Jesus, why is it that the more I love and do for my fellow-man, the more abundantly You seem to give to me?

Trust in the Lord, and do good; so you will dwell in the land, and enjoy security. Take delight in the Lord, and he will give you the desires of your heart.

Psalm 37:3, 4

It's amazing and incredible,
But it's as true as it can be
God loves and understands us all
And that means you and me.
His grace is all-sufficient
For both the young and old,
For the lonely and the timid,
For the brash and for the bold.
His love knows no exceptions,
So never feel excluded,
No matter who or what you are
Your name has been included.
And no matter what your past has been,
Trust God to understand,
And no matter what your problem is
Just place it in His Hand.
For in all of our unloveliness
This great God loves us still,
He loved us since the world began
And what's more, He always will!

No matter who or what we are, what we have done or what we have failed to do, You love us, God, and You always will.

You shall give to him freely, and your heart shall not be grudging when you give to him; because for this the Lord your God will bless you in all your work and in all that you undertake. For the poor will never cease out of the land; therefore I command you, You shall open wide your hand to your brother, to the needy and to the poor, in the land.

Deuteronomy 15:10, 11

So let us give ourselves away
Not just today but every day.
And remember a kind and thoughtful deed
Or a hand outstretched in time of need
Is the rarest of gifts, for it is a part
Not of the purse but a loving heart.
And he who gives of himself will find
True joy of heart and peace of mind.

Lord, whatever talent You have given to me, let me willingly share it with others. Help me to discover the service You desire for me to do and for which I was created.

For if you forgive men when they sin against you, your heavenly Father will also forgive you. But if you do not forgive men their sins, your Father will not forgive your sins.

Matthew 6:14, 15 NIV

Since God forgives us,
we, too, must forgive
And resolve to do better
each day that we live
By constantly trying
to be like Him more nearly
And to trust in His wisdom
and love Him more dearly.

Jesus, I firmly desire to imitate You. Breathe into me the capability to do so.

"Peace be within your walls, and security within your towers!" For my brethren and companions' sake I will say, "Peace be with you!"

Psalm 122:7, 8

Everybody, everywhere, no matter what his station,
Has moments of deep loneliness
    and quiet desperation,
For this lost and lonely feeling
    is inherent in mankind
It is just the Spirit speaking as God tries again to find
An opening in the worldly wall
    man builds against God's touch,
For he feels so self-sufficient
    that he does not need God much.
But the answer keeps eluding him
    for in his selfish, finite mind
He does not even recognize that he cannot ever find
The reason for life's emptiness
    unless he learns to share
The problems and the burdens
    that surround him everywhere
So open up your hardened hearts
    and let God enter in
He only wants to help you a new life to begin.
And this can only happen when you realize it's true
That everyone needs someone
    and that someone is you!

Father, help me to tear down "worldly walls" and build "bridges of understanding" between peoples' hearts. Let the bridges be open to all traffic with no road blocks or detours.

Then Peter came up and said to him, "Lord, how often shall my brother sin against me, and I forgive him? As many as seven times?" Jesus said to him, "I do not say to you seven times, but seventy times seven."

Matthew 18:21, 22

It does not take a new year
To make a brand-new start,
It only takes the deep desire
To try with all your heart
To live a little better
And to always be forgiving
And to add a little sunshine
To the world in which we're living.

Develop within me the quality of forgiveness, Master. May I always keep You as a pattern of how to forgive others for a wrong that has been done.

For now we see in a mirror dimly, but then face to face. Now I know in part; then I shall understand fully, even as I have been fully understood. So faith, hope, love abide, these three; but the greatest of these is love.

1 Corinthians 13:12, 13

God, grant us hope
and faith and love—

Hope for a world
grown cynically cold,
Hungry for power
and greedy for gold.

Faith to believe
when within and without
There's a nameless fear
in a world of doubt.

Love that is bigger
than race or creed,
To cover the world
and fulfill each need.

My loving Jesus, I want so much to have the ability to see You not only in neighbors but in strangers, not only in family members but in those not my relatives, not only in friends but in those who are unfriendly to me. I humbly ask Your help.

And whoever gives to one of these little ones even a cup of cold water because he is a disciple, truly, I say to you, he shall not lose his reward.

Matthew 10:42

Take a cup of kindness
mix it well with love,
Add a lot of patience
and faith in God above.
Sprinkle very generously
with joy and thanks and cheer—
And you'll have lots of "angel food"
to feast on all the year.

Master, permit me to live my life in a manner that is more like a recipe for a well-blended, sweetly flavored, light and airy angel food cake, rather than a mixture of cement which is thoroughly mixed up and permanently set.

So put away all malice and all guile and insincerity and envy and all slander. Like newborn babes, long for the pure spiritual milk, that by it you may grow up to salvation; for you have tasted the kindness of the Lord.

1 Peter 2:1–3

Kindness is a virtue
    given by the Lord,
It pays dividends in happiness
    and joy is its reward.
For, if you practice kindness
    in all you say and do,
The Lord will wrap His kindness
    around your heart and you.
And wrapped within His kindness
    you are sheltered and secure
And under His direction
    your way is safe and sure.

"May I help you?" is a beautiful-sounding question. Dear Lord, permit it to roll frequently from my lips and heart.

The Legend of the Valentine

We love, because he first loved us. If any one says, "I love God," and hates his brother, he is a liar; for he who does not love his brother whom he has seen, cannot love God whom he has not seen. And this commandment we have from him, that he who loves God should love his brother also.

1 John 4:19–21

The story of Saint Valentine
Is a legend, it is true,
But legends are delightful
And very lovely, too.

And the legend of Saint Valentine
Imprisoned in a cell
Thinking of his little flock
He had always loved so well
And, wanting to assure them
Of his friendship and his love,
he picked a bunch of violets
And sent them by a dove.

And on the violets' velvet leaves
He pierced these lines divine
That simply said "I love you"
And "I'm your Valentine."
So through the years that followed
From that day unto this
Folks still send messages of love
And seal them with a kiss.

Because a Saint in prison
Reached outside his bars one day
And picked a bunch of violets
And sent them out to say
That faith and love can triumph,
No matter where you are,
For faith and love are greater
Than the strongest prison bar.

I remember the story of the five loaves and two fishes. Love is like that. Love multiplies when given away. Jesus, teach me to love.

Praise

I will extol the Lord at all times; his praise will always be on my lips. My soul will boast in the Lord; let the afflicted hear me and rejoice. Glorify the Lord with me, let us exalt his name together.

Psalm 34:1–3 NIV

Special poems for special seasons
    are meaningful indeed,
But daily inspiration
    is still man's greatest need.
For day by day all through the year,
    not just on holidays,
Man should glorify the Lord
    in deeds and words of praise.
And when the heart is heavy
    and everything goes wrong,
May these daily words for daily needs
    be like a cheery song
Assuring you He loves you
    and that you never walk alone
For in God's all-wise wisdom
    your every need is known!

Every day I praise You, God. I do not know what the future holds in store for me, but I know who holds my future in His hands. It is You, God.

And now, O Lord God, thou art God, and thy words are true, and thou hast promised this good thing to thy servant; now therefore may it please thee to bless the house of thy servant, that it may continue for ever before thee; for thou, O Lord God, hast spoken and with thy blessing shall the house of thy servant be blessed for ever.

2 Samuel 7:28, 29

Lord, show me the way
I can somehow repay
The blessings You've given to me.
Lord, teach me to do
What You most want me to
And to be what You want me to be.
I'm unworthy I know
But I do love You so
I beg You to answer my plea.
I've not much to give
But as long as I live
May I give it completely to Thee!

Lord, I offer You my past—I give You my present—I dedicate to You my future.

How to Find Happiness

Judge not, and you will not be judged; condemn not, and you will not be condemned; forgive, and you will be forgiven; give, and it will be given to you; good measure, pressed down, shaken together, running over, will be put into your lap. For the measure you give will be the measure you get back.

Luke 6:37, 38

Everybody, everywhere seeks happiness, it's true.
But finding it and keeping it seems difficult to do.
Difficult because we think that happiness is found
Only in the places where wealth and fame abound.
And so we go on searching in palaces of pleasure
Seeking recognition and monetary treasure.
Unaware that happiness is just a state of mind
Within the reach of everyone who takes time to
    be kind.
For in making others happy we will be happy, too.
For the happiness you give away returns to shine
    on you.

Dear God, today I resolve to make another person happy. In so doing, I myself shall be happier and the happiness we share will be multiplied. Happiness and peace of mind are choices and must be worked for—not merely found.

Then turning to the disciples he said privately, "Blessed are the eyes which see what you see! For I tell you that many prophets and kings desired to see what you see, and did not see it. . . ."

Luke 10:23, 24

God, open my eyes so I may see
And feel Your Presence close to me.
Give me strength for my stumbling feet
As I battle the crowd on life's busy street,
And widen the vision of my unseeing eyes
So in passing faces, I'll recognize
Not just a stranger, unloved and unknown,
But a friend with a heart that is much like my own.
Give me perception to make me aware
That scattered profusely on life's thoroughfare
Are the best gifts of God that we daily pass by
As we look at the world with an unseeing eye.

Heavenly Father, help me to look for and find You in others. Permit me to live my life in such a fashion that others may look for and find You in me.

For where your treasure is, there will your heart be also.

Luke 12:34

Precious little memories
    of little things well done,
Make the very darkest day
    a bright and happy one,

Tender little memories
    of some word or deed,
Give us strength and courage
    when we are in need,

Blessed little memories
    help us bear the cross
And soften all the bitterness
    of failure and of loss,

Priceless little memories
    are treasures without price,
And through the gateway of the heart
    they lead to paradise.

Thank You, Jesus, for my precious memories of the past and thank You for the promise of what is yet to come. Teach me to relax in these hectic and busy days. Awaken the laughter within me. Reduce the tension. Help me to take time today to build a snowman, or at least make a snowball. If there is no snow, then let me just pretend!

The heavens are telling the glory of God; and the firmament proclaims his handiwork.

Psalm 19:1

Be glad that you've had such a full, happy life,
Be glad for your joy as well as your strife,
Be glad that you've tasted the bitter and sweet,
Be glad that your life has been full and complete,
Be glad that you've walked with courage each day,
Be glad you've had strength for each step of the way,
Be glad for the comfort you've found in prayer,
But be gladdest of all for God's tender care.

God, when I am discouraged, downcast, and depressed let me remember all that You have done for me. The blessings You have sent are too numerous to count!

Every good endowment and every perfect gift is from above, coming down from the Father of lights with whom there is no variation or shadow due to change.

James 1:17

The richest gifts
Are God's to give,
May you possess them
As long as you live,
May you walk with Him
And dwell in His love
As He sends you good gifts
From heaven above.

Every good gift comes from You, Father. Make me aware of these good gifts and fill me with deep appreciation.

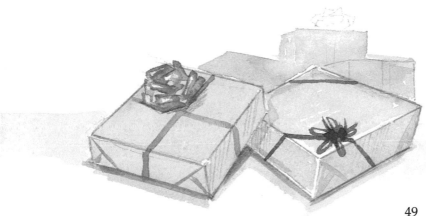

His Likeness Shines Forth

Blessed be the name of the Lord from this time forth
and for evermore! From the rising of the sun to its
setting the name of the Lord is to be praised!

Psalm 113:2, 3

In everything both great and small
We see the hand of God in all,
And every day, somewhere, someplace,
We see the likeness of His face.
For who can watch a new day's birth
Or touch the warm, life-giving earth
Or feel the softness of the breeze
Or look at skies through lacy trees
And say they've never seen His face
Or looked upon His throne of grace.
And man's search for God will end and begin
When he opens his heart to let Christ in.

*Permit me to cordially and courteously greet You, Christ,
and to invite You into my heart and my life.*

The wind blows where it wills, and you hear the sound of it, but you do not know whence it comes or whither it goes; so it is with every one who is born of the Spirit.

John 3:8

In the beauty of a snowflake,
Falling softly on the land,
Is the mystery and the miracle
Of God's great, creative hand!

In the tiny petal
of a tiny flower
that grew from a tiny pod
Is the miracle
and the mystery
of all creation and God!

Whatever the season—winter, spring, summer, or fall—my heart is warm with thoughts of You, Jesus

No Favor Do I Seek Today

Blessed be the Lord! for he has heard the voice of my
supplications. The Lord is my strength and my shield;
in him my heart trusts; so I am helped, and my heart
exults, and with my song I give thanks to him.

Psalm 28:6, 7

I come not to ask, to plead or implore You,
I just come to tell You how much I adore You,
For to kneel in Your Presence makes me feel blest
For I know that You know all my needs best.
And it fills me with joy just to linger with You
As my soul You replenish and my heart You renew,
For prayer is much more than just asking for things—
It's the peace and contentment that quietness
     brings . . .
So thank You again for Your mercy and love
And for making me heir to Your Kingdom above!

*Awaken within me a desire to live my life as a tribute to
You, Almighty Father. All that I am or ever hope to become
is due to You.*

A Sure Way to a Happy Day

He who gives heed to the word will prosper, and
happy is he who trusts in the Lord.

Proverbs 16:20

Happiness is something we create in our mind,
It's not something you search for and so seldom find.
It's just waking up and beginning the day
By counting our blessings and kneeling to pray.
It's giving up thoughts that breed discontent
And accepting what comes as a gift heaven-sent.
It's giving up wishing for things we have not
And making the best of whatever we've got.
It's knowing that life is determined for us,
And pursuing our tasks without fret, fume, or fuss—
For it's by completing what God gives us to do
That we find real contentment and happiness, too.

*Merciful and generous Father, thank You for the blessings
You have sent into my life by way of my faith, my family,
and my friends. Impress upon me that a positive attitude is
also a blessing and well worth the effort to acquire.*

Peace

Jesus Christ is the same yesterday and today and for ever.

Hebrews 13:8

Yesterday's dead, tomorrow's unborn,
So there's nothing to fear and nothing to mourn,
For all that is past and all that has been
Can never return to be lived once again
And what lies ahead or the things that will be
Are still in God's Hands so it is not up to me
To live in the future that is God's great unknown,
For the past and the present God claims for His own,
So all I need do is to live for today
And trust God to show me the truth and the way
For it's only the memory of things that have been
And expecting tomorrow to bring trouble again
That fills my today, which God wants to bless
With uncertain fears and borrowed distress
For all I need live for is this one little minute,
For life's here and now and eternity's in it.

Yesterday is yesterday while today is here, today is today until tomorrow appears, tomorrow is tomorrow until today is past, but Jesus is with us as long as eternity will last. Supreme Giver of Peace, perfect my trust in You.

The Mighty One, God the Lord, speaks and summons the earth from the rising of the sun to its setting. Out of Zion, the perfection of beauty, God shines forth.

Psalm 50:1, 2

Most of the battles
of life are won
by looking
beyond the clouds
to the sun,
and having
the patience
to wait for the day
when the sun comes out
and the clouds
float away!

When the timing is not right for me to have sunshine in my life, give me patience to wait until the sunbeams return. May Your love always shine down on me, my Everlasting Lord.

Lord, Teach Us to Be Patient

Fear not, for I am with you, be not dismayed, for I am your God; I will strengthen you, I will help you. I will uphold you with my victorious right hand.

Isaiah 41:10

Despite unrest around us
Give us quietness of mind,
Teach us to be patient
And help us to be kind,
Give us reassurance
That You are always near
To guide us and protect us
In this violent world of fear,
Help us all to realize
There is untold strength and power
When we seek the Lord and find Him
In our meditation hour.

Father, may I always appreciate the value that comes with stillness of mind and spirit, the calm that comes to me through Your strength and the power of Your silent, spiritual Word.

Every word of God proves true; he is a shield to those who take refuge in him.

Proverbs 30:5

In the center of the flame
   there is a hollow place
And nothing can burn
   in this sheltered space.
For the fire builds a wall
   scientific fact claims
And insures a safe area
   in the midst of the flames.
And in the hurricane's fury
   there's a center of peace
Where the winds of destruction
   suddenly cease.

And this same truth prevails
in life's tribulations
There's an island of calm
in the soul's meditations.
A place that is quiet
where we're shielded from
harms
Secure in the haven
of a kind Father's arms
Where the hot flames of anger
have no power to sear
And the high winds of hatred
and violence and fear
Lose all the wrath
and their savage course
Is softly subdued
as faith weakens force.
So when the fires of life
burn deep in your heart
And the winds of destruction
seem to tear you apart
Remember God loves you
and wants to protect you.
So seek that small haven
and be guided by prayer
To that place of protection
within God's loving care.

*Merciful God, You are the peaceful haven to which I run
when the storms of life set in; please stretch wide Your
loving arms as the refuge into which I can run.*

My Resting Place and My Protection

Thou dost keep him in perfect peace, whose mind is
stayed on thee, because he trusts in thee. Trust in the
Lord for ever, for the Lord God is an everlasting rock.

Isaiah 26:3

God, be my resting place and my protection
In hours of trouble, defeat, and dejection . . .
May I never give way to self-pity and sorrow,
May I always be sure of a better tomorrow,
May I stand undaunted come what may
Secure in the knowledge I have only to pray
And ask my Creator and Father above
To keep me serene in His grace and His love!

*I want to trust You completely, Lord, but how easily I
weaken. Give me strength. Let me know that with You at
my side, I can face today and all the tomorrows.*

For I know the plans I have for you, says the Lord, plans for welfare and not for evil, to give you a future and a hope. Then you will call upon me and come and pray to me, and I will hear you.

Jeremiah 29:11, 12

Refuse to be discouraged,
Refuse to be distressed,
For when we are despondent
Our lives cannot be blessed,
For doubt and fear and worry
Close the door to faith and prayer,
For there's no room for blessings
When we're lost in deep despair.
So remember when you're troubled
With uncertainty and doubt
It is best to tell our Father
What our fear is all about.
For unless we seek His guidance
When troubled times arise
We are bound to make decisions
That are twisted and unwise.
But when we view our problems
Through the eyes of God above,
Misfortunes turn to blessings
And hatred turns to love.

Calm me, Lord. Quiet these fears within me. Stay with me in my search for the peace and harmony that comes from knowing You.

Comfort

. . . he broke them with hard labor; they fell and none could help them rise again. Then they cried to the Lord in their troubles, and he rescued them!

Psalm 107:12, 13 TLB

Trouble is something no one can escape,
Everyone has it in some form or shape—
Some people hide it way down deep inside,
Some people bear it with gallant-like pride,
While others rebel and become bitter and old
With hopes that are dead and hearts that are cold.
But the wise man accepts whatever God sends,
Willing to yield like a storm-tossed tree bends,
Knowing that God never makes a mistake,
So whatever He sends they are willing to take.
For trouble is part and parcel of life
And no man can grow without trouble and strife,
So blest are the people who learn to accept
The trouble men try to escape and reject,
For in our acceptance we're given great grace
And courage and faith and the strength to face
The daily troubles that come to us all
So we may learn to stand straight and tall.
For the grandeur of life is born of defeat
And in overcoming we make life complete.

Father, open my heart to the realization that what makes me strong and capable of finding happiness in this life is not the absence of trials and troubles but rather the growth of my ability to cope with those problems.

There is a river whose streams make glad the city of God, the holy habitation of the Most High. God is in the midst of her, she shall not be moved; God will help her right early.

Psalm 46:4, 5

Take me and break me and make me, dear God,
Just what you want me to be.
Give me the strength to accept what you send
And eyes with the vision to see
All the small arrogant ways that I have
And the vain little things that I do,
Make me aware that I'm often concerned
More with myself than with You.
Uncover before me my weakness and greed
And help me to search deep inside
So I may discover how easy it is
To be selfishly lost in my pride.
And then in Thy goodness and mercy
Look down on this weak, erring one
And tell me that I am forgiven
For all I've so willfully done.
And teach me to humbly start following
The path that the dear Savior trod
So I'll find at the end of life's journey
A home in the city of God.

Most High, in my travels toward the city of God, help me to think first of serving You and then others. Keep me humble. True humility will develop as I give of myself in service.

What Is Life?

Truly, truly, I say to you, he who hears my word and believes him who sent me, has eternal life; he does not come into judgment, but has passed from death to life.

John 5:24

Life is a sojourn here on earth
Which begins the day God gives us birth,
We enter this world from the great unknown
And God gives each spirit a form of its own
And endows this form with a heart and a soul
To spur man on to his ultimate goal.
And through the senses of feeling and seeing,
God makes man into a human being,
So he may experience a mortal life
And through this period of smiles and strife
Prepare himself to return as he came,
For birth and death are in essence the same,
For both are fashioned by God's mighty hand
And, while we cannot understand,
We know we are born to die and arise
For beyond this world in beauty lies
The purpose of living and the ultimate goal
God gives at birth to each seeking soul.
So enjoy your sojourn on earth and be glad
That God gives you a choice between good things
    and bad,
And only be sure that you heed God's voice
Whenever life asks you to make a choice.

Whenever I have a choice to make, Lord, permit me to consult You and listen to Your voice before making the decision.

And he who does not take his cross and follow me is
not worthy of me. He who finds his life will lose it,
and he who loses his life for my sake will find it.

Matthew 10:38, 39

We all have our Gethsemanes
And our daily cross to bear
And we, too, have a Father
We can go to with our care.
A Father who will listen
As He listened to His Son,
And give us strength to carry on
Until life's work is done.

*Jesus, help me to pick up my cross and shoulder it in the
manner that makes You proud of me. Certainly, You have
been a model in teaching us how to carry a cross.*

But he said to me, "My grace is sufficient for you, for my power is made perfect in weakness." I will all the more gladly boast of my weaknesses, that the power of Christ may rest upon me. For the sake of Christ, then, I am content with weaknesses, insults, hardships, persecutions, and calamities; for when I am weak, then I am strong.

2 Corinthians 12:9, 10

Many trials and troubles
Are scattered on our way,
Daily little crosses
Are a part of every day.
But the troubles we have suffered
Are over, passed, and through,
So why should bygone happenings
Keep on gravely troubling you?
And the problems that beset us
In the now and present hour
We need not try to solve alone
Without God's grace and power
And those scheduled for tomorrow
Still belong to God alone—
They are still unborn and formless
And a part of the unknown.
So let us face the trouble
That is ours this present minute,
And count on God to help us
And put His mercy in it.

Gracious God, help me to remember that each day is a new day and I must forget the hurts of yesterday.

Jesus answered him, "If a man loves me, he will keep my word, and my Father will love him, and we will come to him and make our home with him. He who does not love me does not keep my words; and the word which you hear is not mine but the Father's who sent me."

John 14:23, 24

We all need words to live by,
To inspire us and guide us,
Words to give us courage
When the trials of life betide us.
And the words that never fail us
Are the words of God above,
Words of comfort and of courage
Filled with wisdom and with love.
They are ageless and enduring
They have lived through generations,
There's no question left unanswered
In our Father's revelations.
And in this ever-changing world
God's words remain unchanged,
For though through countless ages
They've been often rearranged,
The truth shines through all changes
Just as bright today as when
Our Father made the universe
And breathed His life in men

HOLY
BIBLE

And the words of inspiration
That I write for you today
Are just the old enduring truths
Said in a rhythmic way.
And if my borrowed words of truth
In some way touch your heart,
Then I am deeply thankful
To have had a little part
In sharing these God-given lines,
And I hope you'll share them, too,
With family, friends, and loved ones
And all those dear to you.

Loving Savior, soften my responses to others. Keep back the sharp and quick retorts. Let only charitable thoughts and actions come from me today.

Life Is Eternal

For the wages of sin is death, but the free gift of God is eternal life in Christ Jesus our Lord.

Romans 6:23

If we did not go to sleep at night
We'd never awaken to see the light,
And the joy of watching a new day break
Or meeting the dawn by some quiet lake
Would never be ours unless we slept
While God and all His angels kept
A vigil through this "little death"
That's over with the morning's breath.
And death, too, is a time of sleeping,
For those who die are in God's keeping
And there's a "sunrise" for each soul,
For life not death is God's promised goal.
So trust God's promise and doubt Him never
For only through death can man live forever!

My Loving Savior, let me trust You implicitly. It is true that by dying we indeed are born to eternal life.

. . . I have learned, in whatever state I am, to be content.

Philippians 4:11

> Blessings come in many guises
> That God alone in love devises,
> And sickness which we dread so much
> Can bring a very healing touch,
> For often on the wings of pain
> the peace we sought before in vain
> Will come to us with sweet surprise
> For God is merciful and wise.
> And through long hours of tribulation
> God gives us time for meditation,
> And no sickness can be counted loss
> That teaches us to bear our cross.

Merciful God, when will I learn that daylight does come after the darkness of night and that You give me the ability to turn a cross into a crown?

So we do not lose heart. Though our outer nature is wasting away, our inner nature is being renewed every day. . . . we look not to the things that are seen but to the things that are unseen; for the things that are seen are transient, but the things that are unseen are eternal.

2 Corinthians 4:16, 18

Nothing really ever dies
That is not born anew,
The miracles of nature
All tell us this is true.
The flowers sleeping peacefully
Beneath the winter's snow
Awaken from their icy graves
When spring winds start to blow.
And little brooks and singing streams,
Icebound beneath the snow,
Begin to babble merrily
Beneath the sun's warm glow.
And all around on every side
New life and joy appear
To tell us nothing ever dies
And we should have no fear,
For death is just a detour
Along life's wending way
That leads God's chosen children
To a bright and glorious day.

The bulbs of the springtime lilies go to rest in the winter only to bloom again come spring. I need never worry, for if You have flowers rise from their wintry grave, will You not assist me to do the same?

For as the Father raises the dead and gives them life,
so also the Son gives life to whom he will.

John 5:21

The crackling flames rise skyward
    As the waving grass is burned,
But from the fire on the veld
    A great truth can be learned.
For the green and living hillside
    Becomes a funeral pyre,
As all the grass across the veld
    Is swallowed by the fire.
What yesterday was living,
    Today is dead and still,
But soon a breathless miracle
    Takes place upon the hill.
For, from the blackened ruins
    There arises life anew
And scarlet lilies lift their heads
    Where once the veld grass grew.
So once again the mystery
    Of life and death is wrought,
And man can find assurance
    In this soul-inspiring thought,
That from a bed of ashes
    The fire lilies grew,
And from the ashes of our lives
    God resurrects us, too.

*Lord, help me to recall that dying is merely my being born
again into the beginning of my eternal life.*

Season of Joy

For to us a child is born, to us a son is given; and the government shall be upon his shoulder, and his name will be called "Wonderful Counselor, Mighty God, Everlasting Father, Prince of Peace."

Isaiah 9:6

Our Father up in heaven,
    long, long years ago,
Looked down in His great mercy
    upon the earth below
And saw that folks were lonely
    and lost in deep despair
And so He said, "I'll send My Son
    to walk among them there.
So they can hear Him speaking
    and feel His nearness, too,
And see the many miracles
    that faith alone can do . . .
For if man really sees Him
    and can touch His healing hand
I know it will be easier
    to believe and understand."
And so the Holy Christ Child
    came down to live on earth
And that is why we celebrate
    His holy, wondrous birth,
And that is why at Christmas
    the world becomes aware
That heaven may seem far away
    but God is everywhere.

Jesus, inspire me to put into practice at least some of that which You have taught.

This is how the birth of Jesus Christ came about. His mother Mary was pledged to be married to Joseph, but before they came together, she was found to be with child through the Holy Spirit.

Matthew 1:18 NIV

All the world has heard the story
    of the little Christ Child's birth,
But too few have felt the meaning
    of His mission here on earth.
Some regard it as a story
    that is beautiful to hear,
A lovely Christmas custom
    that we celebrate each year.
But it is more than just a story
    told to make our hearts rejoice,
It's our Father up in heaven
    speaking through the Christ Child's voice,
Telling us of Heavenly Kingdoms
    that He has prepared above
For all who trust His mercy
    and live only for His love . . .
And only through the Christ Child
    can man be born again,
For God sent the Baby Jesus
    as the Savior of all men.

Radiant Baby Jesus, so tiny but so filled with love and peace and joy, let some of Your attributes spill over into my life and abide in me. Help me in turn to share Your generosity and reflect Your munificence to those around me.

"Blessed is the King who comes in the name of the Lord! Peace in heaven and glory in the highest!"

Luke 19:38

If there had never been a Christmas
    or the Holy Christ Child's birth,
Or the angels singing in the sky
    of promised peace on earth—
What would the world be like today
    with no eternal goal,
What would the temporal body be
    without a living soul?
Just what would give us courage
    to push on when hope is dead,
Except the Christmas message
    and the words our Father said—
"In love I send My only Son
    to live and die for you,
And through His resurrection
    You will gain a new life, too."

Thank You, Father, for sending Jesus into our world to show us the way and to tell us of eternal glory.

. . . and a little child shall lead them.

Isaiah 11:6

God sent the little Christ Child
So man might understand
"That a little child shall lead them"
To that unknown "Promised Land"
For God in His great wisdom
Knew that men would rise to power
And forget His holy precepts
In their great triumphal hour.
He knew that they would question
And doubt the Holy Birth
And turn their time and talents
To the pleasures of this earth.
But every new discovery
Is an open avenue
To more and greater mysteries,
And man's search is never through.
For man can never fathom
The mysteries of the Lord
Or understand His promise
Of a heavenly reward.
For no one but a little Child
With simple faith and love
Can lead man's straying footsteps
To higher realms above!

Father, let my faith in You be simple, true, and childlike.

Let All Men Rejoice

And there were shepherds living out in the fields nearby, keeping watch over their flocks at night. An angel of the Lord appeared to them, and the glory of the Lord shone around them, and they were terrified. But the angel said to them, "Do not be afraid. I bring you good news of great joy that will be for all the people."

Luke 2:8–10 NIV

Glad tidings herald the Christ Child's birth—
"Joy to the World" and "Peace on Earth"—
"Glory to God"
let all men rejoice
And hearken once more to the angel's voice.

It matters not who or what you are,
All men can behold the Christmas Star.
For the star that shone is shining still
In the hearts of men
of peace and goodwill,
It offers the answer to every man's need,
Regardless of color or race or creed.

So, joining together in brotherly love,
Let us worship again our Father above,
And forgetting our own little
selfish desires
May we seek what the Star of Christmas
inspires.

Jesus, I join the shepherds as well as the Wise Men in worshiping you. I thank You that You have chosen all kinds of people to be a part of Your family.

"Therefore the Lord himself will give you a sign. Behold, a young woman shall conceive and bear a son, and shall call his name Immanuel."

Isaiah 7:14

Miracles are marvels
That defy all explanation
And Christmas is a miracle
And not just a celebration
For when the true significance
Of this so-called Christmas story
Penetrates the minds of men
And transforms them with its glory,
Then only can rebellious man
So hate-torn with dissension
Behold his adversaries
With a broader new dimension
For we can only live in peace
When we learn to love each other
And accept all human beings
With the compassion of a brother.

And it takes the Christ of Christmas
To change man's point of view
For only through the Christ Child
Can all men be born anew,
And that is why God sent His Son
As a Christmas gift of love
So that wickedness and hatred
Which the world had so much of,
Could find another outlet
By following in Christ's way
And discovering a new power
That violence can't outweigh.
And in the Christmas story
Of the Holy Christ Child's birth
Is the answer to a better world
And goodwill and peace on earth.

The miracle of Christmas has marvelously survived the test of time and shall continue to survive throughout all eternity! We praise You, Father, Son, and Holy Spirit, and we thank You for Mary and for the role that she played.

And suddenly there was with the angel a multitude of the heavenly host praising God and saying, "Glory to God in the highest, and on earth peace among men with whom he is pleased!"

Luke 2:13, 14

"Glory to God in the highest
And peace on earth to men,"
May the Christmas song
the angels sang
Stir in our hearts again
And bring a new awareness
That the fate of every nation
Is sealed securely in the hand
Of the Maker of Creation.
For man, with all his knowledge,
His inventions and his skill,
Can never go an inch beyond
The Holy Father's will.
For all of man's achievements
Are so puny and so small,
Just anthills in the Kingdom
Of the God who made us all.
For, greater than the scope of man
And far beyond all seeing,
In Him who made the universe,
Man lives and has his being.

How can I be an instrument of peace today? With Your guidance, God, I'll find a way.

And she gave birth to her first-born son and wrapped him in swaddling cloths, and laid him in a manger, because there was no place for them in the inn.

Luke 2:7

All over the world at this season,
Expectant hands reach to receive
Gifts that are lavishly fashioned,
The finest that man can conceive
For, purchased and given at Christmas
Are luxuries we long to possess,
Given as favors and tokens
To try in some way to express
That strange, indefinable feeling
Which is part of this glad time of year
When streets are crowded with shoppers
And the air resounds with good cheer.
But back of each tinsel-tied package
Exchanged at this gift-giving season,
Unrecognized often by many,
Lies a deeper, more meaningful reason.
For, born in a manger at Christmas
As a gift from the Father above,
An Infant whose name was called Jesus
Brought mankind the gift of God's love
And the gifts that we give have no purpose
Unless God is part of the giving,
And unless we make Christmas a pattern
To be followed in everyday living.

No place for You in the inn? Welcome to my heart. I want to keep a favorable spot always ready for You, Jesus.

And they went with haste, and found Mary and Joseph, and the babe lying in a manger.

Luke 2:16

Long, long ago in a land far away,
There came the dawn
of the first Christmas day,
And each year we see the promise reborn
That God gave the world
on that first Christmas morn.
For the silent stars in the timeless skies
And the wonderment
in a small child's eyes,
The Christmas songs the carolers sing,
The tidings of joy
that the Christmas bells ring
Remind us again of that still, silent night
When the heavens shone
with a wondrous light,
And the angels sang of peace on earth
And told men of
The Christ Child's birth—
For Christmas is more than a beautiful story,
It's the promise of life
and eternal glory.

Light my path, my Savior, so that I can see in my search to find You.

. . . Then, opening their treasures, they offered him gifts, gold and frankincense and myrrh.

Matthew 2:11

As once more we approach
    the birthday of our King—
Do we search our hearts
    for a gift we can bring,
Do we stand by in awe
    like the small Drummer Boy
Who had no rare jewels,
    not even a toy,
To lay at Christ's crib
    like the Wise Men of old
Who brought precious gifts
    of silver and gold—
But the Drummer Boy played
    for the Infant Child
And the Baby Jesus
    looked up and smiled,
For the boy had given
    the best that he had
And his gift from the heart
    made the Savior glad.

Infant Christ Child, guide me in my selection of a proper gift for You. May the giving of myself, the sharing of my talents, the practice of doing the best that is within me be an acceptable offering. My package will not be wrapped in holiday paper or tied with fancy ribbons. I am the package and the enclosure card reads, "To Jesus with Love."

And the shepherds returned, glorifying and praising God for all they had heard and seen, as it had been told them.

Luke 2:20

At Christmas time our hearts reach out
To friends we think of dearly
And checking through our friendship lists,
As all of us do yearly,
And though we've been too busy
To keep in touch all year,
We send a Christmas greeting
At this season of good cheer.
So Christmas is a lovely link
Between old years and new
That keeps the bond of friendship
Forever unbroken and true.

Glorious Savior, I praise You, I glorify You in song at this season. Let my actions also sing of my love for You and all my friends. Encourage me to create a happy happening that will be a basis for a lovely memory.

All this took place to fulfill what the Lord had said through the prophet: "The virgin will be with child and will give birth to a son, and they will call him Immanuel"—which means, "God with us."

Matthew 1:22, 23 NIV

The joy and wonder
    in children's eyes,
The ageless awe
    in the Christmas skies,
The nameless joy
    that fills the air,
The throngs that kneel
    in praise and prayer.
These are the things
    that make us know
That men may come
    and men may go,
But none will
    ever find a way
To banish Christ
    from Christmas Day.
For with each child
    there's born again
A mystery that baffles men.

Immanuel, encourage me to act in a responsible and responsive manner. At all times may my actions be the kind that are pleasing to You. I desire to live my life in a Christlike manner. To help me accomplish this goal, please, "God be with me."

New Beginnings

A New Year Meditation

I can do all things in him who strengthens me.

Philippians 4:13

What better time and what better season,
What greater occasion or more wonderful reason
To kneel down in prayer and lift our hands high
To the God of creation who made earth and sky,
Who sent us His Son to live here among men
And the message He brought is as true now as then.
So at this glad season when there's joy everywhere
Let us meet our Redeemer at the altar of prayer
Asking Him humbly to bless all of our days
And grant us forgiveness for our erring ways.
And though we're unworthy, dear Father above,
Accept us today and let us dwell in Thy love
So we may grow stronger upheld by Thy grace,
And with Thy assistance be able to face
All the temptations that fill every day,
And hold onto our hands when we stumble and
    stray.
So thank You, dear God, for the year that now ends
And for the great blessing of loved ones and friends.

*Jesus, to You who strengthens me daily, I offer all my days
and all my praise.*

Both riches and honor come from thee, and thou rulest over all. In thy hand are power and might; and in thy hand it is to make great and to give strength to all. And now we thank thee, our God, and praise thy glorious name.

1 Chronicles 29:12, 13

Whatever the new year has in store
Remember there's always a good reason for
Everything that comes into our life,
For even in times of struggle and strife
If we but lift our eyes above
We see our cross as a gift of love.
For things that cause the heart to ache
Until we feel that it must break
Become the strength by which we climb
To higher heights that are sublime.
So welcome every stumbling block
And every thorn and jagged rock,
For each one is a stepping-stone
To a fuller life than we've ever known,
So let us accept what the new year brings,
Seeing the hand of God in all things.

Father, what I do with the rocks that are strewn on my pathway of life depends upon my attitude and ability to cope. I can create stepping-stones to walk upon or I can stumble and fall. Give me your hand as I advance by way of the stepping-stones.

. . . Behold, now is the acceptable time; behold, now
is the day of salvation.

2 Corinthians 6:2

We stand once more
on the threshold
of a shining and unblemished year,
Untouched yet by time and frustration,
unclouded by failure and fear.
How will we use the days of this year
and the time God has placed in our hands?
Will we waste the minutes
and squander the hours,
leaving no prints behind in time's sands?

God, grant us the grace
as another year starts
to use all the hours of our days,
Not for our own selfish interests
and our own willful, often-wrong ways.
But teach us
to take time for praying
and to find time
for listening to You
So each day is spent
well and wisely
doing what You want us to do.

*Time is a gift from You, God; let me not waste it, but let me
use it wisely in serving You and my fellowman and thus in
preparing for eternity.*

Wilt thou not revive us again, that thy people may rejoice in thee? Show us thy steadfast love, O Lord, and grant us thy salvation.

Psalm 85:6

It doesn't take
a new year
to begin our lives anew.
God grants us
new beginnings
each day
the whole year through.
So never be discouraged
for there comes daily
to all men
the chance to make
another start
and begin all over again!

Creator of the universe, You demonstrate to us with the dawning of each day, that we too have an opportunity to start again.

And the Word became flesh and dwelt among us, full of grace and truth; we have beheld his glory, glory as of the only Son from the Father.

John 1:14

As we start a new year
untouched and unmarred,
Unblemished and flawless,
unscratched and unscarred,
May we try to do better and
accomplish much more
And be kinder and wiser
than in the year gone before.
Let us wipe our slates clean
and start over again,
For God gives this privilege to all sincere men
Who will humbly admit they have failed many ways
But are willing to try and improve these "new days"
By asking God's help in all that they do
And counting on Him to refresh and renew
Their courage and faith when things go wrong
And the way seems dark
and the road rough and long.
What will you do
With this year that's so new?
The choice is yours—God leaves that to you!

Father, grant me the perseverance to keep my resolution to be kinder and wiser. Enable me to reach out to the destitute, the hungry, the poor—the forgotten. Let me have loving and helping hands that readily reach out to others.

Be gentle and ready to forgive; never hold grudges. Remember, the Lord forgave you, so you must forgive others.

Colossians 3:13 TLB

God grant us this year a wider view
So we see others' faults through the eyes of You.
Teach us to judge not with hasty tongue,
Neither the adult . . . nor the young,
Give us patience and grace to endure
And a stronger faith so we feel secure,
And instead of remembering, help us forget
The irritations that caused us to fret,
Freely forgiving for some offense
And finding each day a rich recompense
In offering a friendly, helping hand
And trying in all ways to understand
That all of us, whoever we are,
Are trying to reach "an unreachable star."
For the great and small . . . the good and bad,
The young and old . . . the sad and glad
Are asking today, "Is life worth living?"
And the answer is only in loving and giving—
For only love can make man kind
And kindness of heart brings peace of mind,
And by giving love we can start this year
To lift the clouds of hate and fear.

Prince of Peace, help me to view all people through my heart. May I always welcome heartily each new neighbor to our street. Let me be a neighbor to them regardless of their outward appearance.

A New Year! A New Day! A New Life!

May you be strengthened with all power, according to his glorious might, for all endurance and patience with joy, giving thanks to the Father, who has qualified us to share in the inheritance of the saints in light. He has delivered us from the dominion of darkness and transferred us to the kingdom of his beloved Son, in whom we have redemption, the forgiveness of sins.

Colossians 1:11–14

Not only on New Year's
but all the year through
God gives us a chance to begin life anew.
For each day at dawning we have but to pray
That all the mistakes that we made yesterday
Will be blotted out and forgiven by grace,
For God in His love will completely efface
All that is past and He'll grant a new start
To all who are truly repentant at heart.
And well may man pause in awesome-like wonder
That our Father in heaven
who dwells far asunder
Could still remain willing to freely forgive
The shabby, small lives we so selfishly live
And still would be mindful of sin-ridden man
Who constantly goes on defying God's plan—
But this is the gift
of God's limitless love,
A gift that we all are so unworthy of,
But God gave it to us and all we need do
Is to ask God's forgiveness and begin life anew.

Forgive me, Father, for my mistakes. Permit me to start my life anew as this new year begins.

If you found any beauty in the poems of this book
Or some peace and comfort in a word or line
Don't give me praise or worldly acclaim
For the words that you read are not mine . . .
I borrowed them all to share with you
From our Heavenly Father above,
And the joy that you felt was God speaking to you
As He flooded your heart with His love.

H.S.R.

And if you receive any hope or strength
from the Scripture or from the prayer
Just know that whenever or wherever
you read this, our Heavenly Father is there.

V.J.R.